Lots of hats

Harry Hat Man has lots of hats.

He has hats for hens.

He has hats for cats ...

and hats for rats.

He has hats for bats.

He has hats for hippos …

... and a hat that's flat!

Seven eggs

By Lyn Wendon

Eddy Elephant met a red hen.

The red hen had seven eggs!

"Can I have an egg?" said Eddy.

"No, no!" said the red hen.

"Can I sit on the eggs?" said Eddy.

"No, no, no!" said the red hen.

"Well, well, well!" said Eddy.

Go to bed!

By Katie Carr

Go up to bed, Ben.

Is Ben in bed?

No, Ben is not in bed!

Go to bed, Ben.

Is Ben in bed?

Yes, Ben is in bed.

But look at Ben!

Look at the mess!

By Katie Carr

"Shut the door, Mike!" said his Mum.

"Look at all the mess!" she said.

"Go and get the mop," said Mum.

Mike got the mop.

Then Mum's mug fell on the mat!

"Look at the mess!" said Mike.

"Get the mop, Mike!" said Mum.

Sit, Nip!

By Katie Carr

Nick and Nip like to play.

But Nip can dig!

Nip digs and digs.

"Bad dog," says Nick.

"Come to me, Nip," says Dad.

"Sit, Nip," says Dad.

Nip sits!

Pups in the pond

By Katie Carr

"It's hot," says Peter.

Then Peter sees a pup.

Peter plays with the pup.

They run and jump.

They puff and pant.

They plod up to the pond.

Jump! Splash!